AM YOW THE
COMIC?

To Brenda, my wife, to whom I am
indebted for help and advice.

AM YOW THE
COMIC?

Memoirs of a
Black Country Comedian

Peter Bullock

BREWIN BOOKS

BREWIN BOOKS
56 Alcester Road,
Studley,
Warwickshire,
B80 7LG
www.brewinbooks.com

Published by Brewin Books 2019

A CIP catalogue record for this book is available from the British Library.

ISBN: 978-1-85858-597-0

Printed and bound in Great Britain
by 4edge Ltd.

CONTENTS

Acknowledgements

I should like to thank the following for supplying and giving permission to use photographs in this book:

The British Music Hall Society
Birmingham Central Library
Trevor Clarke
Frank Jennings
Brewin Books Ltd
Ned Williams of Uralia Press, Wolverhampton
    (for his Chris Medley photograph)
Keith Hodgkins (for his Alan Price photographs)

Chapter 1

THE BEGINNING

Have you ever, in an idle moment, wondered how many children might have been great musical instrument virtuosos if they'd had the good fortune to have been taught to play an instrument when they were young? Or how many football-mad youngsters would have been Olympic medalists in hockey or judo if they'd only been introduced to the sports when young? Just how many people, I wonder, have a great inborn talent for something that they didn't know they had and, one day, discover it? You need luck, I suppose.

In my case I didn't discover that I had a natural ability to imitate people's voices until I was in Secondary School, during the 1940s. We spent a lot of time, my classmates and I, larking about, making fun of the teachers behind their backs (we didn't dare do it to their faces) and, to my surprise, I found that I could imitate their voices with great accuracy, which amused my classmates no end and gave me a very gratifying kudos in my class.

Actually, I'd always been fascinated by the comedians I'd heard on the radio all through my childhood. The radio was always on in our house (we didn't have a television until I was nearly 18) and I became a great fan of Variety shows such as *Variety Bandbox, Variety Fanfare* and *Blackpool Night*, and I still feel the same excitement at the corny introduction to *Blackpool Night*, "Come where the stars are always bright; be gone dull care, it's Blackpool Night". I lapped up radio comedy shows such as Tommy Handley's *Itma, Take it from Here* (which starred Jimmy Edwards, Dick Bentley and June Whitfield) and *Educating Archie*, which not only starred a ventriloquist's dummy, Archie Andrews (on a radio programme!) but also introduced us to several future stars: Max Bygraves, Tony Hancock and Robert Moreton, to name but three.

By the time I was 16 I found that I could imitate the voices of quite a few well-known comedians, so I exchanged amusing my classmates with impressions of our teachers and started telling them jokes in the voices of the comedians we all heard on the radio. As time went on I increased my repertoire of voices to: Vic Oliver, Ken Platt, Bernard Miles and so on. As soon as I started the catchphrases of my favourites: Ken Platt: "I won't take my coat off, I'm not stopping"; Robb Wilton: "The day war broke out..."; Arthur English: "Open the cage!" I and my school friends had a great deal of fun, and I became very popular as a party guest!

In 1952 it came to me suddenly one day that if I could work up a proper "act" containing all my impressions and using jokes that I'd heard on the radio (stealing other comedians' jokes, in the time-honoured tradition!) I might be able to make some money out of this unexpected talent. I tried out my ideas at parties that my friends invited me to, learning how to cope with an audience, not just consisting of people I knew, but of strangers. I remember once going to a party at a large house in posh Handsworth Wood to do a show, and feeling like a gatecrasher when I realised that I didn't know any of the other people there.

Luckily for me, I could not only imitate voices, but I had a great ability to remember a large number of jokes; even today, if necessary I could still recall hundreds of jokes. Like every other comedian, I wrote down jokes in

Tommy Handley and ITMA.

Peter Brough with 'Archie Andrews'.

Robb Wilton.

Terry Thomas.

Vic Oliver, George Robey and Cyril Fletcher recording at the BBC.

my little joke book. The late, great Bob Monkhouse outdid everybody else with his gargantuan collection of jokes; my little book had only 800+, mostly written in short form, with only the "punch-line" to remind me of the joke.

Not long ago, when I was moving house and collecting up all my belongings, I found the battered little red joke book and I discovered that in the back of the book I'd written a list of all the voices I could do. Comedians: Robert Moreton, Vic Oliver, Ken Platt, Bernard Bresslaw, Ted Lune, Terry-Thomas, Charlie Chester, Max Wall, Chic Murray, Robb Wilton, Jimmy Wheeler, Arthur English, Max Miller, Reg Dixon, Cyril Fletcher, Alfred Marks, Kenneth Horne. Broadcasters: Raymond Glendenning, Ralph Wightman and the Radio Doctor.

Enough material there for a few shows!

But, of course, every performer has to learn how to perform and, at the beginning, friends' parties were only the start of me learning my trade. The next occasion for dipping my toe in the water of show-business came at a friend's wedding. To my surprise, my fledgling act went down well and afterwards I was approached by a fellow guest (no, not Lew Grade!) who asked me to do a turn at our local youth club. Youth clubs in those days were more often than not run by local churches and the members frequently put on entertainment to raise money for the church or for local charities.

I appeared quite regularly at these entertainment evenings, but I was really only appearing before people I knew, friends and neighbours, who wanted me to do well. What I really needed was to try my luck in front of people who didn't know me. The first opportunity came to do that in the early 1950s. In those days, so soon after the war, with all its privations, people were determined to be entertained, not just by the cinema but by live entertainment, which they could go to with the friends and neighbours they had become so close to during the war. At this time Birmingham Council used to hold talent contests in August in some of the big parks. These contests took place in large marquees on two evenings a week and the winner of each evening's contest at all the venues, went forward to the final.

My local park, Handsworth, held such contests, with the final held at Handsworth Park on the evening of the Birmingham Show, which took place on the first Saturday in September. Wishing to stretch my little wings a bit I entered and, to my surprise, I won the "heat" and went forward to the final, along with about 20 other acts from all over Birmingham.

Because of the large number of acts, each performer only had about eight minutes to impress the judges. Most of the finalists were singers, who could easily fit three songs into their eight minutes. For comedians it was a bit harder. They had to build a rapport with their audience in a very short time, so I just chose what I thought were the best bits of my act and hoped for the best. I was quite pleased to come 4th – the first four were considered to be winners and I received a small cash prize, exactly what, I can't remember. The main thing that stuck in my mind about my first outing performing before strangers had nothing to do with the contest itself – it was the strong smell of grass, trodden down and wet, that permeated the whole of the marquee!

Buoyed up by having had a small success in a competition, when we were visiting some ex-neighbours who had gone to live in Brean in Somerset, I entered a similar talent contest held in Weston-Super-Mare. It was held in the grand venue of the Rozel Bandstand, an attractive art-deco building with a covered curved stage and a two-tier auditorium, the top tier of the audience sitting in the open air. Luckily, the evening was fine and the audience large. One of the acts, a comedian from Evesham, just told a long string of jokes. Unfortunately, he went on before me and one of the jokes in his string was one I had been intending to tell, so I had to think of another joke before it was my turn. The little red joke book came in useful then and it was good training for the future as other, much more famous, comedians were to show.

Some years later, Jimmy Tarbuck, at the Royal Variety Performance told a joke that had already been told earlier in the show – either

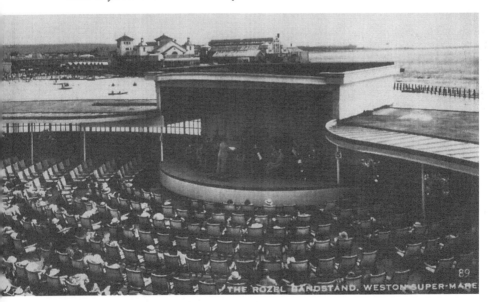

The Rozel Bandstand, Weston-Super-Mare.

unknowingly or in a moment of forgetfulness. When he suddenly realised what he had done, he covered up his mistake magnificently by telling the audience, with a knowing smile, that he had just been checking that they were paying attention to the show, which got him an extra laugh!

Anyway, my finding another joke at a moment's notice seemed to do the trick. I won the contest and received a £1 note as a prize, which in the 1950s was a large sum of money for a youngster. On a later visit to our friends in Brean I entered another talent contest in Weston, this one being held at the luxurious venue of the Winter Gardens Ballroom. The place was packed with holiday-makers, eager to be entertained. This was by far the largest audience I had appeared before, but I came First. This was only a 'heat', however, and my success meant that I could attend the grand final, some three weeks later. What a disappointment! I was only on holiday and would not be in Weston in three weeks' time because my country called – I was due to join the RAF for my two years of National Service, and didn't think a talent contest in Weston would be thought sufficiently important

The Winter Gardens, Weston-Super-Mare.

for me to go AWOL before I'd even joined my unit! The only consolation was that I'd found out that I could cope with a large audience without making a fool of myself.

Actually, the RAF gave me many unexpected opportunities to hone my act as I spent a lot of spare time entertaining my fellow squaddies. As you might expect, their favourite impression was that of our much-hated Corporal, who had made our lives a misery during our eight weeks' stint

Why should England fear? Myself in RAF (second airman from left) in 1957.

at RAF Padgate, Warrington, where we were being transformed into fine RAF men.

As we neared the end of our eight weeks of ritual humiliation, the Corporal invited us to celebrate the end of the torture by an outing to a local pub for a party. After a march of several miles to this 'local' pub, which was in Leigh, we finally found the place. It boasted a tiny stage, where the resident pianist performed. Of course, you know what happened next – I was encouraged (forced!) to go up on the stage to do my act, which had (so my 'friends' said) to include my impression of the Corporal. Fearing dire consequences for this act of insubordination, I did as requested and waited for the axe to fall.

It's possible that the monstrous Corporal had a spark of humour or humanity in him after all, or perhaps he couldn't be bothered to give out one last punishment, but the next day I was, of course, sent for and to my surprise I was asked to repeat my act on the last night of our training for all the Corporals in the Corporals' Mess. Was I being set up? I had no way of knowing but I had to agree. To my relief I needn't have worried after all, for I received a great reception from the Corporals and the next day I left Padgate with a kindlier opinion of the NCO's than they really deserved.

Chapter 2

VARIETY AND ME:
THE BIRMINGHAM HIPPODROME

People these days always seem to dismiss the 1950s as being dull and boring, a dreary, monochrome era, but not for me they weren't. True, my love of Variety acts and comedians in particular was fed by radio programmes and I learnt how to imitate the voices of my favourite comedians by hearing them on the radio, but during the late 40s and the 50s the big holiday resorts, led by Blackpool, all had theatres where they put on summer Variety shows, starring all the favourite artistes whom we had all listened to during the war and afterwards, and holidaymakers flocked in their thousands to see them in the flesh.

Blackpool, in the 1940s and 50s had nine theatres, putting on summer season shows: the three piers; the Winter Gardens; the Opera House; the Queen's; the Hippodrome (an ABC cinema in the winter); the Palace and the Grand (which usually had a popular farce for the season). Each show would run from June to the end of the Blackpool Illuminations in October, a considerable run for any artistes appearing. Blackpool had regulars who appeared season after season, such as comedian Dave Morris and singer Josef Locke. Such regulars often lived in Blackpool.

In addition to the theatres there was, of course, the famous Blackpool Tower Circus, with the resident clown, Charlie Caroli. Many other big seaside resorts had summer shows too, but Blackpool, with its nine theatres was the 'entertainment' capital of Britain. Apart from the play at the Grand, the other Blackpool theatres were run as Variety Theatres, with shows twice nightly, at 6.15 and 8.30. To fit in with this, Blackpool boarding houses served high tea at 5pm, in case their guests wanted to attend the first house at the theatre.

In some of the boarding houses you might find that a fellow guest was someone from a summer show, staying there for the season, someone fairly low on the bill, who couldn't afford to stay at a large hotel. However, someone once told me that the famous pianist, Semprini ("old ones, new ones, loved ones, neglected ones") preferred to stay at a boarding house for the season because it was cosier and he liked the company of the holidaymakers! If I wanted to see my idols, however, I didn't need to go the seaside.

I was lucky enough to have a colourful window into showbusiness and the great artistes of the day: the singers, the comedians, the American superstars, the dancers, the novelty acts (who were to delight us many years later in Jimmy Perry's series called *Turns* which opened our eyes to all those acts from long ago). Yes, I had the best of entertainment – I had the Birmingham Hippodrome.

At the youth club I attended I had a friend, a young man who worked for a film company and who, because of his job, *Alberto Semprini, 1954.*

Exterior of the Hippodrome as it looked from 1899 until demolition of front section and tower during 1963.

received a complimentary ticket for the Birmingham Hippodrome every week. As he wasn't interested in Variety theatre and he knew I was, he usually gave me his ticket; first house on Monday nights. Variety shows changed weekly at the Hippodrome and were twice nightly: 6.15 and 8.30. Variety shows ran from March to December, leaving January and February for the yearly pantomime or popular touring musicals.

So it was, that for a few years from the early to middle 1950s I saw all the great stars of the age, all the legends we revere so these days. Everything about the Variety theatre fascinated me. I learnt that the final rehearsal before the opening of a show was always rehearsed 'back-to-front'. The star of the show who came on last rehearsed first, so that the star wouldn't have to wait about while the rest of the show was run through. Then the rest of the acts would rehearse in reverse order, finishing with the opening act of the show. The stage, therefore, would be ready, set for the opening of the show and would be left in place, ready for the first house the next day.

What stars I saw there! The reason that I got to see some of the most famous performers of the age was that the Hippodrome belonged to the Moss Empires chain of theatres, the top dog. In the hierarchy of Variety theatres, two chains reigned supreme: first was Moss Empires and next was the Stoll Theatre Group. Moss Empires controlled not only the Birmingham Hippodrome and the most famous Variety theatre of all, the London Palladium, but a string of other theatres in other UK cities. The Stoll Theatre Group owned lesser theatres and had, usually, lesser stars. In our area there were third tier theatres such as the Aston Hippodrome and the Plaza, West Bromwich. Such theatres in smaller towns booked whatever artistes they could.

Actually, this hierarchy of theatres was almost exactly echoed by a hierarchy of cinemas. Cinemas were dominated by three chains of owners: Odeon, Gaumont and ABC. Most cities and town centres had several cinemas in the golden age of the cinema, three of which would be owned by the three major chains. Birmingham had an Odeon and a Gaumont and the Forum, which belonged to ABC. These cinemas showed the films from the major film studios: ABC showed mainly films from the MGM Studio, including the great musicals; Odeons showed mainly the films from Paramount (in fact the Birmingham Odeon was originally called The Paramount).

With a wealth of cinemas in Birmingham, we were spoilt for choice. The top cinemas got the best films and the little suburban cinemas, often privately owned, bought the big films to show much later than they had been seen in the centre of the city, and other films touted to them by representatives of the film companies (such as my youth club friend).

Thus, the entertainment business had a strict hierarchy and I was a beneficiary of this, getting to see many of the great performers of the age. Most of the American great entertainers appeared at the London Palladium, but not all of them travelled to the provinces, but even so, I managed to see some of the best.

Some of the great American performers that I saw included Frankie Laine, Guy Mitchell and in 1953 Frank Sinatra, who performed for the whole of the second half of the programme, about 45 minutes, whereas the top artiste usually only did 15-20 minutes. Frank was accompanied by a full British swing band, Billy Ternent and his orchestra. Since about 1950, Frank Sinatra had begun to suffer a fall in his popularity, after years of being a teenage idol 'King of the Bobbysoxers', and the auditorium was only about three quarters full when I saw him. That was about par for the course for first house on a Monday night, but for Frank Sinatra it was unthinkable. Only a year later he appeared in a straight acting part in the film *From Here to Eternity* which brought him back into the public's attention, and from then on, and to this day, he is much revered as, perhaps, "the greatest".

Singers usually topped the bill at Variety theatres, comedians or, at least, British comedians, very rarely topped the bill, usually appearing last but one, according to their appeal and popularity. Someone like Frankie

Howerd was the exception, because he had become such a favourite on radio Variety shows; he appeared accompanied by his female pianist, Madame Blanche Moore, who never spoke and was the butt of his jokes and jibes. Frank suggested confidentially to the audience that she 'wasn't all there' and referred to her, with mock pity as 'poor soul', pleading with the audience not to laugh at her.

Norman Wisdom would soon become a top artiste, enjoying a sudden rise to that position. His act, that of the little man in an ill-fitting suit, put upon or ignored, usually finished with him singing a song, written by himself. When I saw him he sang "Don't laugh at me 'cos I'm a fool" as the lights went out and the curtain came down. A noisy struggle ensued, while he fought his way through the curtain to the front of the stage, then all the house lights went out and he finished his song by the light of a match which he struck and held up to give him at least a bit of light – the little downtrodden man had triumphed and he received a standing ovation.

During the early 1950s I saw comedians, unknown and low on the bill, who later in the decade became big stars, people like Terry Scott, Des O'Connor and Harry Worth. Terry did an act dressed as a naughty young boy in a wolf cub's uniform (shades of Jimmy Clitheroe, who would become a star in later years with his radio series *The Clitheroe Kid*). Harry Worth started as a ventriloquist, and a very funny one, but low on the bill – number three, after the Overture and the opening act. He put on the persona of a nervous newcomer and would say things like, "If you look at the bill outside the theatre, you will see my name – if it's a clear day, that is". Incidentally, he toured the Moss Empires theatres on the same bill as Laurel and Hardy and it was Oliver Hardy who told him that he didn't need to be a ventriloquist with a dummy as he was funny enough on his own. This was certainly true as his television series was a great success.

Yes, I saw that show and felt very privileged to have seen the great (best ever?) comedy duo, Stan Laurel and Oliver Hardy. They came on stage to

Frankie Howerd.

Norman Wisdom.

Harry Worth.

Laurel and Hardy.

their jaunty signature tune, dressed as two burglars, who were attempting to break into a house. They had decided to enter via a sash window, and so came many unsuccessful attempts to push Ollie through the window, with Stan getting more and more concerned when he wouldn't go through. Finally, Ollie went through, whereupon Stan walked calmly to the front door and opened it and walked in; it wasn't locked after all. Of course we knew what would happen, you always did, but their timing was so perfect that you couldn't help laughing.

Happy days and golden memories, but it wasn't only the stars who had my attention. Many of the novelty acts stayed in the mind and some of them became stars in their own right. My favourite were the sand-dancers Wilson, Keppel and Betty, a skeletal trio, dressed as ancient Egyptians, who spread sand on the floor of the stage, then proceeded to shuffle around in line. Betty was between the two men who remained expressionless, silent and never looking towards the audience, as if they had wandered onto the stage accidentally and unnoticed. After this strange performance, they then shuffled offstage leaving the audience in gales of bemused laughter.

Seeing all these acts taught me many a lesson in the art of performance, about the preparation and the execution of a stage act, particularly about the absolute necessity for spot-on timing. And all this invaluable information came to me completely free of charge!

Chapter 3

GET AN AGENT

In the early days of the 1950s I'd had a whale of a time imitating all sorts of people, entering talent contests, building up an act to enable me to take on big audiences and entertain them, but, when, in September 1957, I was demobbed from the RAF, I had some serious decisions to make.

In spite of my enduring love for Variety theatre and my enjoyment in being a comedian/impressionist, it never entered my head at any time to see myself as a top-grade professional entertainer. Not for me the blood, sweat and tears of trying to fight my way to the top of the profession and, once there, having to fight a constant battle to stay there. No, my gift for voices was always going to be a hobby, which brought me great pleasure and a host of precious memories. I was going to spend my working life teaching. To that end, when I left the RAF in September 1957, I went straight to the University of Leicester in October, the first step towards being a teacher of English, which I was for more than 30 years.

That didn't mean, of course, that I wasn't aware that as a poor student, I could do with earning a bit of extra money to see me through the next three years at university. What I needed, allowing me to spend my spare time entertaining people in clubs and pubs, was someone to help me get the bookings I needed.

This was where my early experience came to my aid. A local chap, Fred Hitchens, had seen me perform and he was the Secretary of the Handsworth Social Club. He gave me a leg up by booking me for his club and advised me to join the Birmingham Variety Artistes' Association (the VAA), and kindly recommended me to them. The VAA headquarters was a large, former house in Trinity Road, near to Villa Park and I duly applied to join their ranks. I had been told by Fred that they were the best organisation to help me find weekend work while I was at university, as they had contacts throughout Birmingham and the Black Country, mainly working men's clubs, ex-servicemen's clubs, pubs, Labour and Liberal clubs and, rarely, Conservative clubs. Naturally, there was a small subscription to be paid to join, but the RAF had paid me a month's wages on my demob, so I was able to afford it, and became a professional performer at last.

So, there I was – a member of a real artistes' club. The VAA headquarters had a bar and relaxation rooms which on Thursday evenings and Sunday lunchtimes were thronged with artistes, hoping to pick up some engagements from the club Secretaries who came to engage artistes for their weekend shows. Most clubs had concerts on Saturday and Sunday nights, a few on Sundays only.

Most venues booked three artistes at a time, who would be expected to do two spots of about 15-20 minutes each and variety was the name of the game. A typical bill would consist of a tap-dancing act, a comedian and a singer, although any one of these might be replaced by a magician or instrumentalist. Two 15-20 minutes spots would, of course, be a simple task for a vocalist, who could just sing a few popular songs, or for dancers, but I was rather worried about just how much material a comedian would use up in that time. As I was going to university I worked out that if I could, on some weekends, have two bookings, I could attend the VAA on Sunday lunchtime to try to obtain some bookings for the following weekend. What I would earn for my two shows – £5 (i.e. £2.10s for each) would be enough to pay my fare home and to make a little profit. I couldn't come home every weekend, but I could make up my store of cash by working during the university vacations – about 22 weeks a year. I would, of course, be leading a rather strange double life: spending the weekdays sitting in lectures, writing literary essays for my tutors on the greats of English Literature and the weekends regaling an audience in a Black Country pub with jokes by Ken Platt, Ted Lune and the like.

Just before I started at university I appeared in a Showcase at the VAA, a show that allowed new artistes to appear before the Secretaries from other social clubs. Most of my fellow artistes in this "Showcase" were singers, who sang the latest popular songs, trying to emulate their favourite performers. Through all my years appearing in the local clubs and pubs, the majority of my fellow performers were vocalists, who, pretty well without exception, were pleasant, competent but lacked that vital spark of originality, which might make them a star. Comedians were very much thinner on the ground than singers; indeed I only ever met one other comedian/impressionist like myself, so I had a head-start in getting bookings, by virtue of rarity. As was the custom "Showcase" shows usually included a veteran entertainer to finish the night off. In my "Showcase" show we had a rather elderly comedian, Billy Carlyle, who told jokes that today, would be considered distinctly non-PC.

Any artiste who had a free date on a Sunday night would go to the VAA on Sunday lunchtime and write his/her name on a black-board, hoping to get a booking for that evening. One very fussy comedian I met used to fill his diary with phantom bookings, in case he was asked to appear at a venue he didn't fancy: he would open his diary, stuffed full of "bookings" and turn down the offer with feigned regret. To be honest, I found that most of the venues were much of a muchness and there really was no need to be quite so fastidious!

The author performing in a club.

In the 1950s the Midlands audiences tended to be well-behaved, appreciative and encouraging. However, in the bigger, more professional clubs in the North, particularly in the 1960s, not only were the performers ignored when the time came for the pies to be sold, but many artistes came in for some very rough treatment. Of course, there were many top professional venues which even the stars would not visit. One such was the Glasgow Empire, where, it was said, "if they like you, they let you live!" Although this rarely applied to artistes from England, Max Miller when he was asked why he never played the Glasgow Empire was said to have replied, "I'm a comedian, not a missionary."

Luckily for me the worst I ever experienced was at the Hatherton Liberal club in Walsall. This audience, polite, quiet and respectful, merely sat in silence, unmoved by anything I said and just clapped politely when I finished and left the stage. I wondered afterwards if they had all been deaf!

Although most bookings in my area were made through the VAA, they did not have a monopoly in the field. I had dealings with two independent agents in Birmingham, who specialised in providing artistes for certain clubs and pubs. One of these was called Will Bent, a small, bespectacled man, who always wore a trilby, even indoors. He rented a room in a pub near Snow Hill station on Thursday evenings and Sunday lunchtimes, and booked artistes almost entirely for work in Black Country pubs. He was known as the "thirty bob merchant" as the fee he paid was always £1.10s, a pound less than that paid by the VAA. He would audition a newcomer briefly and, if he was satisfied, he would give him/her a single booking and then, surreptitiously, he would secrete himself in the audience at the venue to watch the artiste work, before offering any other bookings.

Artistes often popped in to see him on their way to the VAA, but Will was not fond of people who just 'popped in'. He preferred artistes to stop and talk over a drink for about half an hour before he offered them any work. It rankled with him to be considered inferior to the VAA, so, if you wanted work from him, it didn't pay to mention the VAA. Presumably the pubs paid him to find performers for them, but it didn't pay to allude to that either when chatting to him.

The other agent I had dealings with was David Kenton, a rather superior person, who also rented a pub room (in Great Charles Street), at the same time as Will Bent. He only had a few artistes on his books, so I counted myself lucky to have found acceptance. Mr Kenton did not audition his acts himself: he initially offered them an unpaid engagement for a charity show and then sat in the audience to judge how well the artiste performed. He didn't, as I remember, provide artistes for pubs; he supplied to clubs, usually more up-market clubs with good facilities and each show paid £3 or more. There were not many of theses clubs, so I was grateful to have passed muster, although I couldn't rely on regular engagements from him. Unlike Will Bent, he did not encourage familiarity with his artistes. He was not unfriendly, but professional and aloof, being generally addressed by his artistes as Mr Kenton.

Most of the artistes were part-time professionals, like myself. They had ordinary jobs during the week and performed only at weekends. There were, however, a small number of full-time professionals who travelled anywhere in the UK where they could get a booking. One such I came across was comedian Bob Hatch, a well-known Birmingham artiste who once performed on a week's Variety bill at the Dudley Hippodrome and whom I once heard on BBC Radio *Blackpool Night*. I also occasionally appeared on the same bill with Alan Randall, a banjo player, who was to find fame with his impressions of George Formby.

One or two Northern cities had clubs which put on shows 6 or 7 days a week. Hull was one of those cities. If you could afford a week's holiday from your day job, you could go up to Hull for a week's engagement. Like all good things, however, there was one major drawback to this – the audiences there consisted mainly of rowdy fishermen who, after a long and arduous time at sea, would have several weeks' wages to spend on drink at the club. I never appeared there, choosing to follow Max Miller's advice about the Glasgow Empire.

In the local venues I played, every show would have a compère, usually the chairman of the club. I was once told about a Chairman, who sat at the side of the stage with his own microphone and who switched off the microphone of the vocalist who was in full flow, rendering him inaudible and then finished the song himself! Comedian Norman Collier used to do a hilarious impression of a self-important Chairman, full of hot air.

When artistes arrived at the venue, they were usually met by the Chairman or Secretary, who often offered a few words of advice on what the audience wanted or expected, "We don't want any swearing or dirty material" or even "They like it a bit rude here." However, sometimes there was quite a mis-match between what the audience wanted and what the artiste had been told.

A Welsh tenor called George Hopkins had in his repertoire classical and operatic arias, but after the end of his first spot in one club, was informed by the Chairman that the customers wanted songs they knew i.e. the latest pop songs, which left George to comment haughtily, "If you want a pop singer, you should book a pop singer!" before carrying on with his classical repertoire in the second half.

Another example of a lack of communication between the Chairman and the artiste involved a young newcomer who finished his first spot, congratulating himself on how well it had gone, only to be told by the Chairman that he had to do a second spot in the second half. Unfortunately, he had nothing left for the second half and so in a blind panic, he fled the scene and hopped on the first train home hoping he wouldn't be missed! For most artistes, however, we just waited for the introduction "Best of order please for..." or "Give a big hand to..." and you were on your own.

In clubs payment was made in cash at the end of the concert; there was no paperwork, just a sealed brown envelope passed over. In pubs you would be paid out of the till, sometimes informally by the barman or pub manager who would enquire in a jokey manner, "How much do we owe you, mate?" Of course, all fees were agreed when you accepted the engagement and nobody would ever ask for more than had been agreed and no club or pub would ever offer less than had been agreed, for fear of being blacklisted.

Facilities for the artistes in pubs were generally pretty basic. You performed, perhaps, on a small dais, which had a piano on it where the resident pianist performed, but sometimes your place was just on the floor of the bar and between acts you sat with the other customers. Some pubs offered a "dressing room" for female vocalists to change their dresses between their two appearances, but generally everything was rough and ready – warm, encouraging and very special, for that.

Chapter 4

IN AT THE DEEP END

Having gone through my rather haphazard apprenticeship, learning how to present my act and cope with an audience, October 1957 when I started at university, marked the beginning of my being a real paid comedian, appearing (if only at weekends), at a host of venues in Birmingham and the Black Country and on reflection I enjoyed every minute of it. I often travelled to my engagements by bus and arrived looking like just another customer. When I worked in the pubs, I was generally greeted by the Secretary. At a venue in Willenhall I appeared looking, I suppose, a little unprepossessing to be greeted by the words, "Am yow the comic?" as if there might be some doubt about it.

Yes, I was the comic, but looking back now I realise I was lucky to have been more than this. A comedian talks in his own voice; he reels off a string of jokes that he hopes the audience will like; but he is always himself. But an impressionist can be a whole host of people, all with their own voice, their own accent, their own catchphrases, own clothes and their own characteristic jokes.

I turn my back to the audience, put on one of Arthur English's wide, garishly-coloured, kipper ties and I am the spiv, the wide-boy, a character so familiar to post-war audiences, who was later to be given immortality by Jimmy Perry and David Croft as Pte Walker in *Dad's Army*. Arthur English delivered his lines quickly, just like the spiv, always trying to do someone down:

"I said to my mate, 'Are you superstitious?'"

"No."

"Well lend me £13 quid!"

At the end of his act he rushed off, making himself scarce, with the words, "Open the cage!"

Big, bluff Jimmy Wheeler cantered through his jokes:

"Johnny came in from playing looking filthy."

"What on earth have you been doing?" asked his mum.

"We've been playing farmyard animals," answered Johnny, "I was a pig. But you should see Jimmy: he was a chicken and tried to lay an egg."

Before anyone could object to a joke he headed for the wings with, "Aye, aye! That's yer lot!"

Because audiences love oneliners; I could give them plenty from Chic Murray and Max Wall.

Chic Murray:

"I'm Detective Inspector Dustbin."

"You must be from the Yard."

or

"Your coat's on fire."

"I know, it's a blazer."

Max Wall:

"I'm wearing my Easter tie. It's got egg allover it."

Jimmy Wheeler.

Ted Lune.

"We call my brother 'ice cream' because he's been a way for so long."

Daft, but funny when they told them!

You could never expect anyone to start his act with "I've had another letter from my Mum..." except gormless, North-country lad, Ted Lune. He just stood there, reading excerpts from the latest letter: "I'm writing this letter slow 'cos I know you can't read fast. Mrs Jones has had all her teeth out and a new gas fire put in." The letter always ended with, "God bless you and keep you from your loving mother." It was just the way he told them!

If a joke didn't suit a particular comedian's voice and delivery, I didn't use it, but I had so many instantly recognisable characters on stage with me that I never felt alone and the audience got a whole number of comedians for their money.

The pubs and clubs where I plied my trade were many and varied. In some pubs you sat with the audience when you were not doing your turn and this gave a nice, cosy feeling to the evening. One such pub was the Theatre Vaults in West Bromwich, which had a rather interesting history. It had once been part of a Variety theatre and the front door had once been the entrance to the theatre, which was in existence as a music hall until as late as 1940.

Another cosy pub was the Seven Stars in Tipton, which had a coal fire in the bar where the shows took place. One evening, during a break between the acts, a young lady member of the Salvation Army came in selling *The War Cry*. On seeing her, one wag in the crowd quipped, "Stick 'em on the fire, luv, it's cold in 'ere!" It was just a bit of fun. She was obviously a regular visitor and the customers were generous.

The entrance to the Theatre Vaults public house on the left and the former theatre adjoining it. A Chris Medley photograph from the collection of Ned Williams.

The Seven Stars, Tipton. An Alan Price photograph from the collection of Keith Hodgkins.

The Lost City (now The Drayton). An Alan Price photograph from the collection of Keith Hodgkins.

Another memorable pub was The Lost City in Ocker Hill, near Wednesbury. The customers loved to chat to the artistes, who often used the customers as part of their act. One particular customer was a real 'character': she was a middle-aged lady whose mouth boasted only one single tooth at the front. She encouraged comedians to remark on it and make jokes about it, never taking offence. I complied with her wishes by remarking that she was the first person in her street to have 'central eating', and then referred to her as Mrs Rowntree, as she had 'clear gums' which won great approval from the crowd!

Actually, it could be quite helpful to a comedian to have someone in the audience to help set the atmosphere. I once did a show at the Horn & Trumpet in Bewdley, which also boasted a female 'character' in the audience. Every time I cracked a joke she burst into full-volume shrieks of laughter, which set the rest of the audience laughing too. However, after one particular joke, we all waited for the storm to break, but – silence! Undeterred, I carried on with my act, only to be suddenly interrupted by a gale of raucous howls of laughter – she'd finally got the joke! This, of course, set everybody else laughing again, including me, and my act, you might say, was a roaring success!

Another pub I loved appearing at was the White Swan, in West Bromwich. It had no stage, you just performed on the floor of the bar. Behind you sat a small jazz band, who performed numbers between the acts – and very good they were too! Their superb drummer was Al Morris, who was well-known in the area. His pièce de résistance was a thunderous version of Woody Herman's *Caldonia*, which nearly brought the house down, literally! Sometimes the band was augmented by an accordianist who was known as "Henry sauce-bottle shoulders", his sloping shoulders having been caused by years of accordion playing. Nights in their company were always a treat.

More up-market than the Black Country pubs that made you so welcome was the Farcroft Hotel in Handsworth, a large pub that could accommodate big groups for celebration dinners and the like. Three

The Farcroft Hotel, Handsworth.

artistes were booked for a concert every Saturday night and they performed on a small stage with a resident pianist playing, dressed in a tuxedo and bow tie. It had pretensions, did the Farcroft! All artistes were officially booked into "The Farcroft Music Society" by the Secretary, Albert Tatton. Whether the music society actually existed or not I never discovered, but you felt you had definitely gone up in the world when you appeared there.

I found working in the pubs for not much money most enjoyable but a lot of the artistes preferred to work in the clubs because they often offered better pay and facilities. The Smethwick Labour Club was a typical working-class club and had a large, appreciative audience. The resident pianist, who played before the show started and in the intervals between the acts, was a very fine instrumentalist, obviously of a much higher standard than the usual club pianist. I soon learnt that he was George Coates, brother of the famous Eric Coates, composer of much light music and the music from *The Dambusters* film. George had been a pianist in the pit orchestra at the Birmingham Theatre Royal, but when the theatre closed in late 1956, he became redundant and took up working at the Smethwick Labour Club. One of the evenings when I was there he began the evening playing Ivor Novello melodies. A man sitting near me in the audience grunted in disgust and remarked, "Why is he playing chamber music tonight?" There was, of course, no answer to that.

As you might imagine, pianists varied enormously in quality across the clubs, which was of great importance to the many vocalists who appeared in them. If an artiste couldn't afford to bring his/her own accompanist, he/she was left to the sometimes untender mercy of the club pianist. Many a complaint was heard, if only to fellow artistes, who sympathised.

Certainly, many complaints were heard about the pianist at the Trades Hall in Oldbury, a working-men's club that kept the original name of the building in which it was housed. The man in question, it must be admitted, certainly seemed to play more wrong notes than right ones. When he played the National Anthem at the end of the concert, the tune was only recognizable in a few chords. He once boasted to a long-suffering vocalist whose act he had mangled, that he had written his own arrangement of the anthem and always used his version, "I don't play it like other pianists," he declared proudly, which brought forth from the unfortunate vocalist the time-honoured reply, "You can say that again!"

Two of my favourite clubs were both in West Bromwich: Spon Lane Labour and West Bromwich Labour. I found their audiences an absolute pleasure to play to, but the only drawback, to me, was my popularity always meant that they would ask me to return about three months later. Being a comedian meant that I really preferred to leave a year between repeat engagements because that enabled me to be able to use some of the material that I had used on my last visit!

My dilemma was one that many a professional comedian had, too. If a comedian worked for one of the major theatre chains, he was able to go from town to town appearing at all this chain's theatres in the country, returning to the first one after about a year, so he could use the same material to a different audience. Indeed there were many comedians that hardly changed their material year after year.

With the advent of television by the 1960s, finding new material became a real headache for comedians and quite a few transferred from stand-up comedy to acting in sitcoms, where the words were written for them, or they were forced, like the great Bob Hope, to employ a veritable army of joke writers to keep them supplied with ever new material. As for me, I had to husband my material as best as I could.

I didn't play many up-market clubs, but one such, where I did appear was the Longbridge Social Club, which boasted fine facilities. It had a large stage with spotlights and footlights, along with first-rate sound equipment. The backstage facilities were equally good – a spacious dressing room with comfortable furniture. It had more the feeling of a night club; very different from the homely clubs I usually worked at. My usual clubs were intimate, friendly, but I found the footlights came between me and my audience and I felt a bit ill at ease. However, the audiences were enthusiastic and encouraging, mainly drawn from the Longbridge car factory, who were well paid and expected more from their place of leisure.

These were the years I spent touring the pubs and clubs, never really knowing what I was going to find at each of them – so many clubs, so many unpretentious pubs; so many happy memories.

Chapter 5

LATER YEARS

When I first went up to university, my roommates and new friends, of course, knew nothing of my side-line of being a comedian, but there was a lot of speculation amongst my companions about just what I was up to when I went home for so many weekends during term time. Naturally, it wasn't long before they sussed out that they had amongst them a Variety star!

When I didn't go home for the weekend, I took to going to the Leicester branch of the Variety Artistes' Association, who found me engagements in and around Leicester. Actually, I wasn't the only student who augmented his student grant by doing weekend shows. I was sometimes accompanied on my engagements by a fellow student, called Tony Todd, a vocalist with dark good looks, who specialized in the Dean Martin Italian hits such as *Volare* and *Esso Besso*. Unfortunately, at the end of the year Tony failed his exams and was sent down, leaving me to plough a lonely furrow in Leicester's pubs and clubs.

Perhaps the most unusual booking I got at this time was at the Social Club of a local shoe factory. I imagined I should be working in a typical working-men's club, but when I got there, I found that I was to be doing my act in an actual workshop at the factory, with the audience sitting amongst then machines, facing an improvised stage. I quite enjoyed the unusual experience, as did the audience, which made me think of the BBC *Workers' Playtime* radio broadcasts during and after the war, which must have been recorded in just the same setting as this.

The most public of my appearances at this time, however, came in the university's "Rag Week", a traditional week near the end of term when the students put their minds to raising money for charity, in a series of events and stunts. On the Saturday there was a procession of floats through the town, the university magazine called *Lucifer*, was sold in the streets, although it seems that the title put some people off buying it, for when a student offered a copy to one lady she refused it with the words, "No thank you I am not of that religion".

The most interesting activity to me came in the form of a Variety show, "The Rag Revue", which took place on the Wednesday and Thursday of the Rag Week, in a city centre building, The Corn Exchange, which, considering the material on show there, was a completely appropriate name for the venue!

Tickets were sold in the town as well as to students and both nights saw very big audiences. The major content of the shows were "corn": we had a mock Victorian melodrama, which had the first and last stage appearance of my future wife, playing a Victorian mother. You could understand the sheer horror of it when you read a joke from it:

Mother (to stupid son): "You will have to smarten yourself up. Why don't you put toilet water on your hair?"

Son: "I tried to, Mother, but the seat kept falling on my head."

No wonder my wife felt that the stage was not for her!

Then came a double act, reading out spurious letters:

"Dear Sir, since using your product I am a changed man. Signed Mrs Ivy Gribble." (Which has a modern ring to it, these days!)

"Since using your soap I have used no other!"

'Corn' at The Corn Exchange! (The Rag Revue, 1960).

Of course, the students had to be careful of the content of their performances, for we then were in the age of theatre censorship when the Lord Chancellor's office wielded the dreaded "blue pencil" with abandon and many a great joke was forbidden. Not only did the magazine *Lucifer* have to have an offending page removed before it could be sold to the public, but one of the songs in the parody of the BBC pop programme *Drumbeat* (which we christened *Crumbeat*) was banned altogether. It was called *Sexy Rexy* and it was to be sung by one of the girls. Many years later, when I saw the girl again, she confided that when her mother had found out that she was to sing in public such an "unsuitable song", she had been shocked and was grateful for the Lord Chancellor's blue pencil. How times change!

I didn't get off scot free, either. One of my jokes, to be told as by Ken Platt, was also struck out. It went like this:

"I was on a ship in a storm and everyone was being sick… One of the staff said 'If you feel sick, eat rice pudding'."

"Why? Will it stop me being sick!"

"No, but it looks cleaner on the deck."

What a gem the audience missed!

As a matter of fact I had no reason to be dissatisfied with my act as, not only was it very well received by the audiences, but it received a glowing review in the local newspaper *The Leicester Mercury*. That the review was penned by an old university friend who had just got a job on the local paper had nothing to do with it, of course!

Happy days, but I couldn't be a student forever, and soon I had to do an impression of a pillar of the Establishment, as an English teacher in a local Grammar School. This is where my years of experience facing large audiences came in very useful. Facing a class of 35 fifteen year old boys, all not too keen on learning anything, held no terrors for me. Unfortunately, teaching more than 200 boys a week, preparing lessons, marking their books, as well as coping with marriage and two young children didn't leave me much time to be a comedian.

For some years I taught, produced school plays and coped with the drudgery of marking, and my past life was all but forgotten. But not quite. From time to time I did charity shows just to see if I could still do the voices and please an audience.

There are lots of stories about professional divas, who want roses in their dressing room, or the room painted lilac and so on; there are their male equivalents whose ego knows no bounds, and who behave in odd ways. Actor Ronald Fraser tells the story of when he went to work for actor/director Donald Wolfit, who was noted for his eccentricity. When he asked a new recruit his name, he winced and said, "I shall call you Fraser," muttering darkly, "I have had bad experiences with Ronalds."

In the lower reaches of artistes, where I belonged, there were not many egos on view, but go down further, to the amateur performers and you find people who make life sheer purgatory. There are those who put their fingers in their ears when the leading lady sings and those who, like an old-school union member are all too keen to withdraw their labour at the drop of a hat.

Take dress rehearsals, for example. At one Christmas charity show I appeared in, the final rehearsal began at 2.30pm and I foolishly calculated that it should end about 5.30pm, allowing for a few rough passages to be ironed out. Not so. Proceedings dragged on interminably and after tears, mayhem and a minor revolt, we finished at 10.30pm, leaving the frazzled Director and the least robust performers in a state resembling wrung-out dishcloths. We'd had people forgetting their lines (if they had ever learnt them), coming on stage from the wrong side, speaking their lines from the wings, unseen by the audience, like the disembodied voice of God, all of which gave precious little hope for the success of the show.

Surprisingly enough, the performer that caused the most trouble was a lady whose task was simply to wear a lovely dress and sing *The Holy City*. Unfortunately, it had been decided that in order to make her appearance more dramatic, she was to appear on a dark stage, illuminated by a single spotlight (they only had one spot and the lighting man very obviously had no idea of how to use it). She began singing, stopped after two bars and complained that the spot was in the wrong place: cue frantic adjustments to the spot. This pantomime went on for the next six attempts but, of course, in the end it was more or less right and *The Holy City* got sung. I felt great despair when I thought of the chances of the performance actually working, but naturally, as with all amateur shows, it went off all right and the audience, who, I suppose, hadn't expected much, considered themselves pleased.

Another show I appeared in for charity was *Happy as a Sandbag*, a jolly, nostalgic show that showcased all the hit songs of the Second World War. My contribution to the show was to be a turn as the comedian Max Miller, and a small swing band played Glenn Miller songs, which everybody remembered from the war.

They all, of course, knew Max Miller. He was a giant of the age. He'd first been popular in the 1930s and he remained so until his death in 1963.

Myself as Max Miller.

The Variety theatre was his natural home: he had the audience in the palm of his hand as soon as he came on stage. Indeed, he needed a live audience to be at his best; he even used them in his act. Radio wasn't his medium, partly, I suppose, because his suggestive jokes didn't please the BBC: he wasn't called "the cheeky chappie" for nothing. His cleverness came in implicating the audience in the suggestiveness of the jokes, telling them that they misunderstood the jokes, sullying them with their own far from pure minds reading into them meanings he never intended. I saw him live at the Birmingham Hippodrome and I don't think I ever saw an artiste who was better at controlling and manipulating an audience. Max Miller was the best of them all.

Max Miller as himself!

What was so amazing about this person, "the cheeky chappie", was that offstage Max Miller was nothing like the persona he created on stage. He was a figment of Max Miller's imagination. Just how much respected and loved was the real Max Miller can be seen in this story. He lived in Brighton and didn't like to stay up in London after performing the show every night, so he used to take the train back to Brighton after the show every night. It was said, and I believe it, that if he was a bit late getting to the station one night when the show had run over a little, the train would be delayed for him until he was safely on board. That's star quality!

My last performance (to date!) was in 2014, when I appeared in another nostalgic wartime show, where I was to do my impression of the great wartime comedian and a great favourite of mine, Robb Wilton. He always began his act by saying in his flat, unemotional tones, "The day war broke out…" and told his stories flatly, without emotion, which was hilarious. He spoke about being detailed to wait with a few friends on the white cliffs of Dover, just in case Hitler were to invade.

"My wife said, if Hitler does come, how will you know it's him?"

"Well, I've got a tongue in my head, haven't I?" was the irritated reply! It really was the way he told them that makes him so unforgettable.

Nearly all the comedians that I did impressions of are dead now, remembered only by my contemporaries. Tommy Cooper and Morecambe & Wise have had their memories polished up and refreshed by regular TV reruns of their television shows, but I think it so sad that all the comedians I used to imitate, all different, all real characters, are now almost forgotten. That golden age of radio comedy, the Variety venues, large and small that entertained so many people for so long are only remembered in books, but I wouldn't have missed playing my small part in the story for the world.